ROCKING R[ ]
RECIPES

A Complete Cookbook of Dish Ideas
from Yesteryear!

Table of Contents

There are some outstanding retro desserts you will enjoy preparing – and devouring. Try some of these… *66*

Conclusion *80*

Introduction

How can you bring some retro taste to your meals at home?

Are the ingredients for these vintage dishes still available and easy to find?

Some food traditions seem to continue from one decade to the next, and even from one generation to the next. Recipe cards and word of mouth help to keep retro recipes alive. New recipes are fun to create, but there is something special about recreating the dishes you may have eaten in your youth.

Retro recipes are fun to make, because they bring part of the past into the present. They bring you nostalgic feelings and plenty of smiles to your table. Vintage recipes are a passionate project for some home cooks. It's so easy to find the recipes trending today, but you won't find recipes from older cookbooks as easily.

Some of the retro dishes in this cookbook are more time or labor-intensive than others. Most of them are fairly simple, since in those days we weren't as concerned with dishes having gluten-free, Paleo or other diet-related attributes we cook meals with today.

In the world of retro recipes, you will find meals that were designed around the crops grown at home, and how to stretch the dollar when planning meals. Back then, food was not only about flavor, but about sustenance. Try some of these super recipes soon!

Retro breakfasts are every bit as tasty and filling as the meals we eat most commonly in the morning today. Here are some of the best...

1 – Breakfast Egg Bacon Casserole

This recipe comes from several decades ago. The warm, rich sauce is especially tasty on those cold, dark winter mornings.

Makes 12-16 Servings

Cooking + Prep Time: 1 1/4 hour

Ingredients:

- 1 lb. of sliced then diced bacon
- 2 pkgs. of dried beef, sliced in thin strips

- 1 x 4-oz. can of mushrooms, sliced
- 1/2 cup of flour, all-purpose
- 1/8 tsp. of pepper, ground
- 4 cups of milk, whole
- 16 eggs, large
- 1 cup of milk, evaporated
- 1/4 tsp. of salt, kosher
- 1/4 cup of cubed butter, unsalted
- Optional: chopped parsley, fresh

Instructions:

1. Cook the bacon till crisp in large sized skillet. Remove to plate lined with paper towels. Discard all drippings except 1/4 cup.

2. In same skillet, add mushrooms, beef, pepper and flour to drippings. Cook till combined well. Add milk gradually. Stir while cooking till thickened. Add bacon and stir. Set mixture aside.

3. Whisk evaporated milk, eggs and kosher salt in large mixing bowl. Heat the butter in a separate skillet till it is hot. Add the egg mixture. Stir while cooking on med. heat till eggs have set completely.

4. Place 1/2 of eggs in lightly greased 13" x 9" casserole dish. Pour 1/2 of sauce over eggs. Repeat the layers.

5. Cover casserole dish. Bake in 350F oven for 50-60 minutes, till knife pushed in middle of casserole comes back clean. Allow to stand for five minutes, then serve.

2 – Bran Banana Muffins

These muffins are a long-time classic in many homes. They're an excellent way to make use of those overripe bananas that otherwise might go to waste.

Makes 12 Servings

Cooking + Prep Time: 40 minutes

Ingredients:

- 1/2 cup of softened butter, unsalted
- 1/2 cup of sugar, brown

- 3 mashed bananas, ripe
- 1/4 cup of milk, 2%
- 1 tsp. of vanilla extract, pure
- 2 eggs, large
- 1 1/2 cups of flour, all-purpose
- 1/2 cup of bran, wheat
- 1 tsp. of baking soda
- 1 tsp. of baking powder
- 1/4 tsp. of salt, kosher
- 1/2 cup of walnuts, chopped

Instructions:

1. Preheat the oven to 375F. Grease muffin pan lightly.

2. Cream the butter and the brown sugar till fluffy, in large sized bowl. Add milk, bananas, eggs and vanilla. Combine thoroughly.

3. Add and stir bran, flour, baking soda, baking flour and kosher salt. Blend only till the mixture has become moist. Add and stir walnuts. Pour the batter into the muffin cups.

4. Bake in 375F oven for 20-25 minutes, till toothpick in middle of one muffin comes back clear. Allow the muffins

to sit in cups to cool for about five minutes. Remove and place on wire rack to finish cooling. Serve.

3 – French Toast with Vanilla

This easy but tasty recipe originally came from Mexico. When you first taste them, you'll wonder what **Makes** them especially delicious, if you don't already know they have vanilla in them.

Makes 6 Servings

Cooking + Prep Time: 20 minutes

Ingredients:

- 4 lightly beaten eggs, large
- 1 cup of milk, 2%
- 2 tbsp. of sugar, granulated
- 2 tsp. of vanilla extract, pure
- 1/8 tsp. of salt, kosher
- 12 slices of sandwich bread, day-old
- Toppings, optional: butter, powdered sugar, fresh berries, maple syrup

Instructions:

1. Whisk first five ingredients together in shallow dish. Heat a pre-greased griddle on med. heat.

2. Dip the bread in the shallow dish. Allow it to soak for about 30 seconds per side. Cook on the griddle till golden brown in color on each side. Add toppings, if desired. Serve.

4 – Easy Breakfast Crepes

Crepes look rather distinguished on your breakfast plate, but they are actually basic and simple to make. This recipe creates amazing crepes that taste like sweet, thin pancakes.

Makes 5 Servings

Cooking + Prep Time: 25 minutes

Ingredients:

- 1 cup of flour, all-purpose

- 1 tbsp. of sugar, powdered
- 1/4 tsp. of baking powder
- 1/4 tsp. of salt, kosher
- 1 1/4 cups of milk, 2%
- 1/4 tsp. of vanilla extract, pure
- For the topping
- 5 tsp. of butter, unsalted
- 2 1/2 tbsp. of sugar, powdered

Instructions:

1. Mix the dry ingredients, then add vanilla and milk.

2. Heat a skillet to med-high. Use non-stick spray on it between crepes.

3. Pour 1/2 cup of batter in middle of the skillet. Tilt the pan quickly in all directions to evenly spread out the batter.

4. Cook till crepe doesn't look wet anymore. There is no need to flip and cook the upper side.

5. Remove each crepe to plate and top with 1 tsp. butter. Sprinkle crepes with 1/2 tbsp. of powdered sugar each. Roll them up and top with more sugar, if you like. Serve.

5 – Slow Cooker Apple Spice Oatmeal

These simple oats with the tart taste of apple offer you and your family a cozy, warm breakfast. They are easy to make, even on busy mornings.

Makes 10 Servings

Cooking + Prep Time: 15 minutes + 4 1/2 hours slow cooker time

Ingredients:

- 1/2 cup of brown sugar, packed
- 2 tbsp. of lemon juice, fresh
- 2 tbsp. of molasses, pure
- 3 tsp. of cinnamon, ground
- 1 tsp. of nutmeg, ground
- 1/2 tsp. of ginger, ground
- 1/2 tsp. of allspice, ground
- 1/4 tsp. of salt, kosher
- 4 peeled, sliced apples, medium
- 2 cups of oats, steel-cut
- 2 eggs, large
- 2 1/2 cups of water, filtered
- 2 cups of milk, 2%
- 1 cup of dairy creamer, vanilla, refrigerated
- Optional: extra milk and chopped pecans

Instructions:

1. Mix the first eight ingredients together. Place the apples in lightly greased medium sized slow cooker. Add brown sugar on top of the mixture. Then add oats.

2. Whisk water, eggs, creamer and milk together and pour the mixture over the oats. Cover slow cooker and cook till oats become tender, usually about 4 1/2 hours. Add extra milk and pecans, if desired. Serve.

There are lots of retro recipes for lunches, dinners, side dishes and appetizers. Try some of these soon...

6 – Turkey and Rice Soup

If you have cooked, leftover turkey in your refrigerator, this meal comes together even more quickly. In around a half hour, you'll be enjoying spoons full of goodness.

Makes 6 Servings

Cooking + Prep Time: 35 minutes

Ingredients:

- 1 tsp. of butter, unsalted
- 1 sliced rib of celery
- 1 sliced carrot, medium
- 1/2 cup of chopped mushrooms, fresh
- 2 cups of broth, turkey
- 3/4 lb. of cubed, processed cheese (like Velveeta®)
- 1 1/2 cups of cubed turkey, cooked
- 1 1/2 cups of rice, cooked
- 2 tsp. of granules chicken bouillon
- 1/2 tsp. of celery salt
- 1/4 tsp. of pepper, ground

Instructions:

1. Melt the butter on med-high in large sized sauce pan. Add the mushrooms, celery and carrot. Stir while cooking for six to eight minutes, till veggies are tender.

2. Add and stir broth, turkey, cheese, bouillon, rice, ground pepper and celery salt. Stir while cooking till soup is completely heated and cheese has melted. Serve.

7 – Johnnie Marzetti Pasta

Adults and children alike enjoy this casserole, which is well suited to buffet dinners. There are many recipes for this pasta dish, but this is one of the tastiest.

Makes 6 Servings

Cooking + Prep Time: 2 hours

Ingredients:

- 8 oz. of rotini
- 1 lb. of beef, ground
- 1/2 lb. of bulk Italian sausage, mild
- 3/4 cup of onion, chopped
- 1/4 cup of celery, chopped
- 1 minced garlic clove
- 1 tbsp. of minced bell pepper, green
- Kosher salt ground pepper, as desired
- 1 x 14 1/2 oz. can of tomatoes, diced
- 1 x 15-oz. can of tomato sauce, low sodium
- 2 cups of Italian cheese blend shreds
- 1 1/2 cups of cheddar cheese shreds

Instructions:

1. Preheat the oven to 350F.

2. Bring large sized pot of salted, filtered water to boil. Add the pasta. Cool till barely al dente and drain. Hold colander under running cold water to stop cooking process. Set rotini aside.

3. Cook and crumble the sausage and ground beef till fully browned. Add and mix onion, garlic, celery and bell pepper. Continue to stir while cooking for five more minutes. Season as desired. Remove from the heat. Add and stir tomato sauce and tomatoes. Let the mixture cool for about five minutes.

4. Grease large baking dish lightly. Spread pasta in bottom, covering it evenly. Sprinkle on the Italian blend cheese. Pour meat mixture on pasta cheese.

5. Cover the dish with foil. Bake at 350F for 40-45 minutes. Remove the foil. Sprinkle top of pasta with cheddar cheese shreds. Continue to bake till cheddar melts. Allow the dish to rest for 8-10 minutes and serve.

8 – Monte Cristo Bake

This tasty casserole offers you flavors that seem like they come from both grilled cheese and Monte Cristo sandwiches. They go together wonderfully!

Makes 6 Servings

Cooking + Prep Time: 1 hour 5 minutes

Ingredients:

- 1 1/2 cups of milk, 2%
- 4 eggs, large
- 6 cups of 1/2" bread cubes, French
- 1 x 7 1/2-ounce package of chopped ham, slow cooked
- 1 1/2 cups of Swiss cheese shreds

Instructions:

1. Heat the oven to 350F.

2. Whisk the milk and eggs in a large sized bowl till blended well. Add the bread and stir so that you are evenly coating bread cubes with the egg mixture. Stir in the ham and 1/2 of cheese gently.

3. Spray a 9x9" casserole dish with non-stick spray. Spoon mixture into it. Top with the rest of the cheese.

4. Bake for 40-45 minutes till knife pushed into middle comes back clean. Top should be a golden brown in color. Remove from oven and serve hot.

9 – Pineapple-Orange Chicken

This recipe is easy but still offers great taste. You can add rice while it is simmering, if you like. It comes together quickly, too.

Makes 5 Servings

Cooking + Prep Time: 45 minutes

Ingredients:

- 5 halved chicken breasts, boneless, skinless
- 1 oz. of soup mix, dry, onion
- 2 cups of water, filtered
- 1 x 15-oz. can of drained pineapple
- 1 round-sliced orange, large
- 1 tbsp. of oil, vegetable

Instructions:

1. Spray a large fry pan with non-stick spray. Brown the chicken in the pan on med-high heat, with meat side facing down.

2. Turn the chicken. Add water, pineapple chunks and soup.

3. Cover pan. Reduce the heat down to low and allow to simmer for 1/2 hour. Garnish using round orange slices and cooked chunks of pineapple. Serve.

10 – Italian Meatballs

This recipe goes many years back to Italian families in the United States. It uses turkey and ground beef for the meatballs now, and that **Makes** it a little healthier.

Makes 8 Servings

Cooking + Prep Time: 55 minutes

Ingredients:

- 2 tsp. of oil, olive
- 1 chopped onion, medium
- 3 minced cloves of garlic

- 3/4 cup of bread crumbs, seasoned
- 1/2 cup of grated cheese, Parmesan
- 2 lightly beaten eggs, large
- 1 tsp. each of parsley flakes, dried basil and oregano
- 3/4 tsp. of salt, kosher
- 1 lb. of ground beef, lean
- 1 lb. of ground turkey, lean

Instructions:

1. Preheat the oven to 375F. Heat the oil in skillet on med-high. Add the onion. Stir while cooking till it is tender, which usually takes three to four minutes. Add the garlic and cook for one minute more. Allow to cool a bit.

2. Combine eggs, cheese, onion mixture, bread crumbs and seasonings in large sized bowl. Add the beef and turkey. Mix well but lightly and shape the mixture into 1 1/2" balls.

3. Next, place the meatballs on non-stick sprayed rack. Place in 15"x10"x1" glass casserole dish. Bake at 375F till cooked through and browned lightly, or about 20 to 22 minutes. Remove from oven and serve.

11 – Retro Salmon Loaf

This recipe comes together quickly, since it doesn't have an over-abundance of ingredients. If your mother used to make this, you'll remember the great taste when you experience it again.

Makes 4 Servings

Cooking + Prep Time: 55 minutes

Ingredients:

- 1 x 14 3/4-oz. can of undrained salmon
- 1/2 cup of saltine crackers, crushed
- 1/2 cup of milk, whole
- 1 beaten egg, large
- Kosher salt ground pepper, as desired
- 2 tbsp. of butter, melted

Instructions:

1. Preheat the oven to 350F.

2. Combine salmon, saltine crumbs, egg, milk and the melted butter. Season as desired and mix well.

3. Press salmon mixture into 9"x5" loaf pan.

4. Bake in 350F oven for 40-45 minutes, till done through. Remove from oven and serve.

12 – Simple Meat Loaf

This meat loaf is so easy to make, and a very basic recipe. The tastes blend together in ways you'll remember from long ago.

Makes 8 Servings

Cooking + Prep Time: 30 minutes + 3 hours slow cooker time

Ingredients:

- 2 lightly beaten eggs, large
- 1/2 cup of tomato sauce

- 1/4 cup of ketchup, low sodium

- 1 tsp. of Worcestershire sauce

- 1 chopped onion, small

- 10 saltines, crushed

- 3/4 tsp. of garlic, minced

- 1/4 tsp. of salt, seasoned

- 1/8 tsp. of pepper, seasoned

- 1 1/2 lbs. of ground beef, lean

- 1/2 lb. of pork sausage, bulk, reduced fat

For the sauce

- 1/2 cup of ketchup, low sodium

- 3 tbsp. of sugar, brown

- 1/4 tsp. of nutmeg, ground

- 3/4 tsp. of mustard, ground

Instructions:

1. Cut out three aluminum foil strips measuring 3-inches by 25 inches. Lay them crisscrossed so they look like wheel spokes. Place the strips on bottom and then up sides of medium slow cooker. Coat them with non-stick spray.

2. Combine first nine ingredients in large sized bowl. Crumble the sausage and beef over the mixture. Combine well, creating a moist mixture, and shape it into a loaf. Then place the meat loaf in middle of strips.

3. Combine the sauce ingredients in small sized bowl. Spoon the mixture over the meat load. Cover. Cook on the low setting for three to four hours, till internal temperature is 160F and no pink color remains.

4. Use the strips of foil for handles, removing meat loaf to a serving platter. Serve.

13 – Rainbow Rotini Pasta Salad

This wonderful Italian-inspired pasta salad offers your dinner table a colorful appeal, with its rainbow rotini. The flavor is great too, featuring cheese, broccoli and pepperoni.

Makes 4 Servings

Cooking + Prep Time: 30 minutes + 1 hour refrigeration time

Ingredients:

- 1 x 16-oz. pkg. of rotini pasta, tri-colored
- 1/4-lb. of pepperoni sausage slices

- 1 cup of broccoli florets, fresh
- 1 x 6-oz. can of drained, sliced black olives
- 1 x 8-oz. pkg. of mozzarella cheese shreds
- 1 x 16-oz. bottle of salad dressing, Italian

Instructions:

1. Bring large-sized pot of salted water to boil. Add the pasta. Cook for eight to 10 minutes, till it is done al dente. Drain the pasta and rinse two times in cold, filtered water.

2. Combine the cooked pasta with cheese, olives, broccoli, pepperoni and salad dressing.

3. Refrigerate for an hour or longer and serve.

14 – Classic Pork Chops

These mouth-watering, tender pork chops taste somewhat like a sweet and sour type dish, but they don't need as much time or attention. They go from prep to table in just about a half-hour.

Makes 4 Servings

Cooking + Prep Time: 35 minutes

Ingredients:

- 1/2 cup of pineapple juice, fresh if available

- 2 tbsp. of sugar, brown
- 2 tbsp. of vinegar, cider
- 1/2 tsp. of salt, kosher
- 2 tbsp. of oil, olive
- 4 x 5-oz. pork loin chops, boneless
- 2 chopped onions, medium
- Optional: green onion slices and cooked noodles

Instructions:

1. Mix the first four ingredients together. Heat 1 tbsp. of oil in large sized skillet on med. heat. Brown the pork chops on each side and remove them from the pan.

2. In the same skillet, sauté the onions in the leftover oil, on med. heat, till they are tender. Add the juice mixture and bring to boil. Reduce the heat and cover the pan. Simmer for about 10 minutes.

3. Add the pork chops and cover pan again. Cook till internal temperature is at least 145F, which typically takes two to three minutes. Cover pan again. Allow the chops to stand for about five minutes. Serve on noodles topped with sliced green onions, if you like.

15 – Retro Chicken Pot Pie

This is such an excellent recipe, especially since it's easy to make and you can tweak the taste the way you like it. It tastes just as great re-heated the next day, too.

Makes 6 Servings

Cooking + Prep Time: 45 minutes

Ingredients:

- 1 x 9" double pie crust, prepared
- 1 chopped carrot
- 1 chopped head of broccoli, fresh
- 2 cooked, chopped, halved chicken breasts, boneless
- 1 x 10 3/4-oz. can of condensed soup, cream of chicken
- 2/3 cup of milk, low fat
- 1 cup of cheddar cheese shreds
- 1/2 tsp. of salt, kosher

Instructions:

1. Preheat the oven to 425F.

2. Steam the broccoli and carrots in covered medium pot for three minutes, till firm but a bit tender.

3. Mix soup, chicken, cheese, milk, broccoli, carrots and kosher salt together in large mixing bowl. Spoon this mixture in a pastry-lined 9" pie pan. Cover with the top crust. Seal the edges and slice some cuts in top, to vent the steam.

4. Bake in 425F oven for 1/2 hour, till mixture is a golden brown color. Remove from oven and serve.

16 – Traditional Spanish Rice

For people who enjoy Spanish rice, this is an ultimate type of comfort food. It offers a taste of home, and you can add a bit more chili powder if you want the flavor punched up.

Makes 4 Servings

Cooking + Prep Time: 25 minutes

Ingredients:

- 1 lb. of ground beef, lean
- 1 chopped medium pepper, green
- 1 chopped onion, large

- 1 x 15-oz. can of tomato sauce, reduced sodium
- 1 x 14 1/2-oz. can of drained, diced tomatoes, with no salt added
- 1 tsp. of cumin, ground
- 1 tsp. of chili powder
- 1/2 tsp. of garlic powder
- 1/4 tsp. of salt, kosher
- 2 2/3 cups of brown rice, cooked

Instructions:

1. Cook the beef, pepper and onion in large sized skillet on med. heat, for six to eight minutes. Crumble the beef as it cooks. Beef should have no pink remaining and the onion should be tender. Drain the mixture.

2. Add and stir tomatoes, tomato sauce and the seasonings and bring them to boil. Add the rice and stir occasionally while heating it through. Remove from heat and serve.

17 – Chicken a la King

This is an elegant-appearing chicken dish that is also easy to prepare. The red pimentos and green peppers make it a great Christmas holiday dish, but it is enjoyed year round.

Makes 7 Servings

Cooking + Prep Time: 1/2 hour

Ingredients:

- 1 chopped bell pepper, green
- 1 x 4 1/2-oz. can of drained mushrooms – reserve the liquid
- 1/2 cup of butter, softened
- 1/2 cup of flour, all-purpose

- 1 tsp. of salt, kosher

- 1/4 tsp. of ground pepper, black

- 1 1/2 tsp. of powdered chicken bouillon

- 1 1/2 cups of milk, low fat

- 1 1/4 cups of filtered water, hot

- 4 chopped, cooked, halved chicken breasts, boneless

- 4 oz. of pimento, chopped

Instructions:

1. Stir while cooking the green pepper and drained mushrooms in pan with butter on med. heat for about five minutes. Remove pan from heat.

2. Blend in the kosher salt, ground pepper and flour. Cook on low and stir constantly till mixture has become bubbly. Then remove it from heat.

3. Add and stir water, milk, mushroom liquid and bouillon. Heat till it boils while constantly stirring. Stir and boil for a minute.

4. Add and stir chicken pieces and pimento and heat the mixture through. Remove from heat and serve.

18 – Chicken Tetrazzini

The rotisserie chicken in this recipe **Makes** the baked spaghetti into a cozy, warm meal that your family will love. You can use leftover chicken or even leftover turkey, if you like.

Makes 6 Servings

Cooking + Prep Time: 1 hour

Ingredients:

- 8 oz. of spaghetti, uncooked
- 2 tsp. + 3 tbsp. of butter, unsalted

- 2 chopped strips of bacon
- 2 cups of sliced mushrooms, fresh
- 1 chopped onion, small
- 1 chopped small pepper, green
- 1/3 cup of flour, all-purpose
- 1/4 tsp. of salt, kosher
- 1/4 tsp. of black pepper, ground
- 3 cups of broth, chicken
- 3 cups of rotisserie chicken, shredded coarsely
- 2 cups of peas, frozen
- 1 x 4-oz. jar of diced, drained pimentos
- 1/2 cup of grated cheese, parmesan

Instructions:

1. Preheat the oven to 375F. Cook the spaghetti in pan on med. heat according to instructions on package, till it is done al dente. Drain the spaghetti and transfer it to lightly greased 9x13-inch baking dish. Add 2 tsp. of butter. Toss and coat well.

2. Cook the bacon in large sized skillet on med. heat till it is crisp, moving it occasionally. Then remove it and allow it to drain on a plate lined with paper towels. Discard the drippings except for 1 tbsp. left in pan.

3. Add the mushrooms, green pepper and onion to the drippings. Stir while cooking on med-high for five to seven minutes, till tender. Remove veggies from the pan.

4. In the same pan, warm the rest of the butter on med. heat. Add and stir flour, kosher salt ground pepper, till you have a smooth mixture. Whisk in the broth gradually.

5. Bring mixture to boil and stir occasionally. Stir and cook for three to five minutes, till thickened slightly. Add the pimentos, peas, chicken and the mushroom mixture. Heat the new mixture through while occasionally stirring. Spoon it over the spaghetti and sprinkle the top with bacon and parmesan cheese.

6. Pour mixture into large baking dish. Leave uncovered and bake for 25 to 30 minutes, till it is a golden brown color. Allow to stand for 8-10 minutes and serve.

19 – Retro Tuna Casserole

Even if you have picky eaters in your household, you'll find that this dish is well-received. The chips create a crunchy crust that adds to the appeal.

Makes 6 Servings

Cooking + Prep Time: 40 minutes

Ingredients:

- 1 x 12-oz. pkg. of egg noodles, uncooked
- 1/8 cup of chopped onions

- 2 cups of cheddar cheese shreds
- 1 cup of peas, frozen
- 2 x 5-oz. cans of drained tuna
- 2 x 10.75-oz. cans of creamy condensed soup, mushroom
- 1/2 x 4 1/2-oz. can sliced mushrooms
- 1 cup of potato chips, crushed

Instructions:

1. Bring large sized pot of salted water to boil. Cook the pasta using instructions on package until it is al dente, which usually takes eight to 10 minutes. Drain the pasta.

2. Preheat the oven to 425F.

3. Thoroughly mix noodles, onions, a cup of cheese, tuna, peas, mushrooms and soup in large sized bowl. Transfer mixture to 13" x 9" baking dish. Top with crumbs and last cup of cheese.

4. Bake at 425F for 15-20 minutes till cheese becomes bubbly. Remove from the oven and serve.

20 – Waldorf Salad

This Waldorf salad recipe is super-easy, and it gets its zip from lemon juice. The nuts and apples give it a great crunch, too.

Makes 9 Servings

Cooking + Prep Time: 35 minutes

Ingredients:

- 4 medium chopped apples, 2 each Red Delicious and Golden Delicious
- 2 tbsp. of lemon juice, fresh
- 2 chopped ribs of celery
- 3/4 cup of walnuts, chopped
- 1/2 cup of raisins
- 1 cup of mayonnaise, light
- Optional: ground nutmeg and ground cinnamon

Instructions:

1. Toss the apples in lemon juice in large sized bowl. Stir in mayo, raisins, walnuts and celery gently.

2. Sprinkle with nutmeg and cinnamon, if you like. Refrigerate till you serve it.

21 – Brown Sugar Smoky Links

Smoky links are SO tasty already, and they're even better wrapped in bacon. The brown sugar **Makes** them super sweet. This is a great appetizer for parties and carry-in meals.

Makes 12 Servings

Cooking + Prep Time: 25 minutes

Ingredients:

- 1 lb. of bacon, lean
- 1 x 16-oz. pkg. of little smoked sausages
- 1 cup of sugar, brown + extra if desired

Instructions:

1. Preheat the oven to 350F.

2. Cut bacon slices in thirds. Wrap each small strip around a smoked sausage. Place wrapped sausage links on skewers with two or three on each one. Arrange skewers on cookie sheet. Sprinkle with the brown sugar.

3. Bake at 350F till brown sugar melts and bacon crisps. Serve.

22 – Salisbury Steak

These Salisbury steaks take some time to prepare, for the forming of patties and mixing the ground beef. But the slow cooker does most of the rest.

Makes 6 Servings

Cooking + Prep Time: 20 minutes + 4 hours slow cooker time

Ingredients:

- 1 cup of sliced mushrooms, Baby Portobello
- 1 thinly sliced onion
- 1 1/3 lbs. of ground beef, lean
- 1 tbsp. of seasoning blend, steak
- 3 tbsp. of Worcestershire sauce
- 1 tsp. of onion flakes, dried
- 1 tsp. of parsley, dried
- 1/2 cup of plain bread crumbs
- 1 egg, large
- 3 tbsp. of corn starch
- 2 cups of broth, beef
- 1/8 tsp. of pepper, ground

Instructions:

1. Spray large slow cooker using non-stick spray. Add onions and sliced mushrooms.

2. To prepare ground beef mixture, combine ground beef with bread crumbs, parsley, onion flakes, 1 tbsp. Worcestershire sauce and steak seasoning and mix well.

3. Divide beef mixture in four to six patties. Form patties into oval shapes by pressing on them. Place in slow cooker. Space them out and don't stack them on top of each other.

4. Mix 2 tbsp. of Worcestershire sauce, 2 cups of broth, ground pepper and 2 tbsp. of corn starch together. Whisk till you have a smooth consistency. Pour over beef patties.

5. Place lid on slow cooker. Cook on the High setting for four hours.

6. Once Salisbury steak has completely cooked, remove steaks from slow cooker. Mix 2 tbsp. of water and 1 tbsp. of corn starch in small sized bowl. Stir this mixture into gravy in slow cooker. Mix till it thickens.

7. Add onion and mushroom gravy over Salisbury steaks. Serve on mashed potatoes or egg noodles, if you like.

23 – Sloppy Joes

Here is a perennial favorite – sloppy joes. You will never go back to eating the canned sloppy joe offerings once you've tried this traditional recipe.

Makes 6 Servings

Cooking + Prep Time: 45 minutes

Ingredients:

- 1 lb. of ground beef, lean
- 1/4 cup of onion, chopped
- 1/4 cup of chopped bell pepper, green
- 1/2 tsp. of garlic powder

- 1 tsp. of yellow mustard, prepared
- 3/4 cup of ketchup, low sodium
- 3 tsp. of sugar, brown
- Kosher salt, as desired
- Ground pepper, as desired

Instructions:

1. Brown beef, pepper and onion in skillet on med. heat. Drain off the liquids.

2. Add and stir ketchup, mustard, brown sugar and garlic powder. Mix well. Reduce the heat. Allow to simmer for 1/2 hour. Season as desired. Serve.

24 – Hamburger Pie

The filling of this meat pie pairs quite nicely with the biscuit crust. If you want a fuller dish, you can add some cooked rice to your beef mixture.

Makes 4-6 Servings

Cooking + Prep Time: 40 minutes

Ingredients:

- 1/2 lb. of cooked, drained beef, ground
- 3/4 cup of celery, chopped
- 3/4 cup of onion, chopped

- 2/3 cup of tomato soup, condensed, undiluted
- 1/4 cup of green pepper, chopped
- 1/2 tsp. of salt, kosher
- 2 cups of baking/biscuit mix
- 2/3 cup of milk, low fat

Instructions:

1. Combine first six ingredients in large bowl. Mix thoroughly. Set bowl aside.

2. In separate bowl, toss the milk and baking mix till it forms a soft dough.

3. On lightly floured work surface, roll dough out to fit 9" pie plate. Line the pie plate with the pastry.

4. Fill pie with the meat mixture. Trim flute the edges.

5. Bake in 375F oven for 15-17 minutes, till crust has a golden brown color. Remove and serve hot.

25 – Shrimp Cocktail

If you dine at fine restaurants, you were once greeted by shrimp cocktails as appetizers. They're still as tasty now as they were decades ago.

Makes 4 Servings

Cooking + Prep Time: 55 minutes

Ingredients:

For poaching liquid

- 3 quarts of cold water, filtered
- 1/4 sliced onion
- 1/2 lemon, fresh
- 2 peeled, bruised garlic cloves
- 2 sprigs of tarragon, fresh
- 1 tbsp. of seasoning blend, seafood type
- 1 tsp. of whole peppercorns, black
- 1 bay leaf

For the cocktail sauce

- 1/2 cup of ketchup, low sodium
- 1/4 cup of chili sauce
- 1/4 cup of horseradish, prepared
- 1 tsp. of lemon juice, fresh
- 1 tsp. of Worcestershire sauce
- 3 drops of hot sauce, +/- as desired
- 1 pinch of sea salt
- 2 lbs. of jumbo shrimp, deveined, shells on

Instructions:

1. Stir the water, lemon, onion, tarragon, garlic, peppercorns, bay leaf and seafood seasoning together in large sized pot. Bring it to simmer, then cook till the flavors have blended, which usually takes 12-15 minutes or so.

2. Whisk the chili sauce, ketchup, Worcestershire sauce, hot sauce, lemon juice and sea salt together in separate bowl. Refrigerate for 15 minutes or longer, till the mixture is chilled.

3. Bring the poaching liquid to high boil. Cook shrimp in this liquid till they turn a bright shade of pink outside. Center of shrimp should not be transparent anymore.

4. Immerse shrimp in bowl of filtered ice water till they are cold. Drain them well. Arrange the cold shrimp around platter. Serve with the chilled sauce.

There are some outstanding retro desserts you will enjoy preparing – and devouring. Try some of these...

26 – Classic Tiramisu

This is an elegant dessert that looks as good as it tastes. It features a mascarpone custard that's layered with sweet whipped cream and lady fingers soaked in coffee and rum.

Makes 12 Servings

Cooking + Prep Time: 1 1/4 hour + 5 to 7 hours refrigeration time

Ingredients:

- 6 yolks from large eggs
- 3/4 cup of sugar, granulated
- 2/3 cup of milk, whole
- 1 1/4 cups of cream, heavy
- 1/2 tsp. of vanilla extract, pure
- 1 lb. of cheese, mascarpone
- 1/4 cup of brewed coffee, lukewarm
- 2 tbsp. of rum
- 2 x 3-oz. pkgs. of lady finger cookies
- 1 tbsp. of cocoa powder, unsweetened

Instructions:

1. Whisk egg yolks granulated sugar together in a sauce pan till blended well. Whisk in the milk. Cook on med. heat and stir constantly till mixture reaches a boil. Allow to gently boil for one minute. Then remove pan from heat. Allow it to cool a bit. Cover the pan tightly. Place in refrigerator and chill for an hour.

2. Beat cream and vanilla in medium sized bowl till it forms stiff peaks. Whisk the mascarpone cheese into the yolk mixture till you have a smooth texture.

3. Combine rum and coffee in small sized bowl. Split the lady fingers in halves lengthways. Drizzle them with the coffee and rum mixture.

4. Arrange 1/2 of the soaked lady finger cookies in the bottom of an 11" x 7" dish. Spread 1/2 mascarpone cheese mixture over the lady fingers. Spread 1/2 whipped cream over it next.

5. Repeat the layers. Sprinkle cocoa on top. Cover. Place in the refrigerator for four to six hours, till it sets. Serve.

27 – Butterscotch Pie

The butterscotch in this recipe has a rich flavor that is mellow, so it won't overpower the rest of the pie. It's creamy and smooth, and you get some of each flavor in every bite.

Makes 6-8 Servings

Cooking + Prep Time: 55 minutes + 3-8 hours refrigeration time

Ingredients:

- 1 ready-made pie crust
- 1 cup of sugar, brown, packed
- 1/3 cup of flour, all-purpose
- 2 cups of milk, whole
- 3 egg yolks, large
- 1/4 tsp. of salt, kosher
- 1 tsp. of syrup, maple
- 3 tbsp. of cubed butter, unsalted
- 1/4 cup of sugar, powdered

For whipped cream

- 1 x 8-ounce tub of whipped topping
- 1/4 cup of sugar, powdered

Instructions:

1. Combine the flour, brown sugar, milk, kosher salt and egg yolks in a sauce pan.

2. Cook on med. heat and whisk till the mixture has thickened and is starting to boil. This typically takes between four and six minutes or so. Continue cooking and whisk rapidly for two additional minutes.

3. Remove pan from the heat. Whisk in the maple syrup. Then add in and whisk one piece of butter at a time till they are all in the pan.

4. Pour butterscotch pudding in a medium bowl. Chill over icy water bath. Stir pudding till it cools a little, for two to three minutes.

5. Transfer the pudding to the pie shell. Cover the top with cling wrap. Chill in the refrigerator for a few hours, or overnight.

6. To prepare whipped cream, beat cream in large sized bowl, gradually adding sugar, till it forms soft peaks. Beat further till peaks are almost stiff.

7. Top with the whipped cream after pie cools. Serve.

28 – Lemon Chiffon Retro Pie

This pie is delightful – it's a fluffy and light chiffon pie. You can use lime juice, if you like. Each slice is garnished with sweet whipped cream for extra taste.

Makes 12 Servings

Cooking + Prep Time: 45 minutes + refrigeration till set

Ingredients:

- 1 x 1/4-oz. pkg. of gelatin, unflavored
- 1/4 cup of filtered water, cold
- 4 egg whites, large
- 4 egg yolks, large
- 1 cup of sugar, granulated
- 1/2 cup of lemon juice, fresh
- 1 tsp. of zest, lemon
- 1/2 tsp. of salt, kosher
- 1 x 9" pie crust, prepared

Instructions:

1. Soften the gelatin in filtered water for about five minutes.

2. Beat the egg yolks. Add 1/2 cup sugar, then lemon juice kosher salt.

3. Cook mixture in top of double boiler while constantly stirring, until the consistency is like custard. Add softened gelatin and grated zest of lemon and stir well. Allow to cool.

4. When mixture starts thickening, whip the egg whites till they are stiff. Add the remaining 1/2 cup of sugar as you whip. Fold the egg whites into the custard.

5. Pour the filling into the pie shell. Place in refrigerator and chill till it is firm. Garnish using sweetened whipped cream, as desired. Serve.

29 – Cherries Jubilee

This dessert sounds like a party and tastes divine. It was served at the dawn of the 20th century at the golden jubilee of Queen Victoria of England. The tastes still "wow" people today.

Makes 2-3 Servings

Cooking + Prep Time: 40 minutes

Ingredients:

- 2 tbsp. of butter, unsalted
- 1/2 cup of brown sugar, light, packed

- 1 lb. of stemmed, pitted fresh cherries, or frozen thawed, pitted cherries
- 1 pinch of salt, kosher
- 1 tbsp. of brandy or bourbon
- Lemon juice, fresh
- Ice cream, vanilla

Instructions:

1. Melt the butter in large skillet on med. heat. Add the sugar. Stir till it dissolves. Add the salt and cherries and coat by stirring.

2. Cook the cherries as you stir occasionally, till they release their juices and start reducing a bit. This usually takes 10 minutes or so.

3. Remove the pan from stove top burner. Add and stir brandy or bourbon. Return the pan to burner. Simmer till the juices have thickened. Season as desired with the lemon juice and allow to cool a bit.

4. Spoon the warmed cherry mixture over vanilla ice cream. Serve.

30 – Retro Gelatin Layer "Salad"

This dessert is wonderful as is, and you can add fruit to the layers if you want even more flavor. The dish is especially loved by children, since it's so sweet and colorful.

Makes 18 Servings

Cooking + Prep Time: 1 hour + 5 1/4 hours refrigeration time

Ingredients:

- 7 x 3-oz. pkgs. of Jell-O® fruit gelatin, assorted flavors

- 4 1/2 cups of boiling water, filtered
- 4 1/2 cups of cold water, filtered
- 1 x 12 fluid oz. can of milk, evaporated
- 1 x 8-oz. container of frozen, thawed whipped topping

Instructions:

1. Coat 13" x 9" dish using non-stick spray.

2. Dissolve 1 pkg. of Jell-O® in 3/4 cup of boiling water. Add and stir 3/4 cup of cold water in. Spoon this mixture into the pan. Refrigerate till nearly set, about 45 minutes or so.

3. Dissolve another pkg. of Jell-O® in 1/2 cup of boiling water. Add and stir 1/2 cup of cold water + 1/2 can of evaporated milk. Spoon this over the first layer. Refrigerate till nearly set, again – 45 minutes or so.

4. Repeat steps two and three until you have used all the gelatin. Top with the whipped topping and serve.

Conclusion

This retro cookbook has shown you…

How to use different ingredients to affect unique throwback tastes in dishes you may have heard of or enjoyed, if you're old enough.

How can you include retro dishes in your home recipe repertoire?

You can…

- Make breakfast burritos and egg muffins, just like McDonald's does. They are just as tasty at home.
- Learn to cook with old-style ingredients, which are still readily available in grocery stores in most areas.
- Enjoy making the delectable seafood and meat dishes of yesterday, using salmon, tuna, beef, pork and chicken. Fish and meat are stars in many of these recipes from yesterday.

- Make retro dishes using all kinds of vegetables and fruits, which are still used in so many flavorful recipes.
- Make various types of desserts like cherries jubilee and lemon chiffon pie – they will tempt your family's sweet tooth.

Have fun experimenting! Enjoy the results!

Printed in Great Britain
by Amazon

22196335R00046